Power of Self-Motivation
The Magic of Thinking Big

By Frank Knoll

Disclaimer:

© 2018 - TWK - Publishing. All Rights Reserved.

No part of this publication may be reproduced, stored or transmitted in any form or by any means – electronic, mechanical, scanning, photocopying, recording or otherwise, without prior written permission from the author.

This publication is provided for informational and educational purposes only and cannot be used as a substitute for expert medical advice. The information contained herein does not take into account an individual reader's health or medical history.

Hence, it's important to consult with a health care professional before starting any regimen mentioned herein. Though all possible efforts have been made in the preparation of this e-Book, the author makes no warranties as to the accuracy or completeness of its contents.

The readers understand that they can follow the information, guidelines and ideas mentioned in this eBook at their own risk. All trademarks mentioned are the property of their respective owners.

Table of Contents

Introduction 1
Chapter 1 Creative thought 6
Chapter 2 Develop a big picture 16
Chapter 3 SMART goals 25
Chapter 4 Reflective Thinking 33
Chapter 5 Shared goal or accountability 41
Chapter 6 Bring value to others 48
Chapter 7 Patience and focus 57
Conclusion 66

Introduction

Motivation can be elusive and as unpredictable. It can be non-existent for days on end and it can also appear out of the blue. Staying motivated can be very challenging, especially on days when you need it the most.

But what if instead of waiting for it to come, there's a way for us to sustain our motivational drive? What if instead of wandering aimlessly until motivation comes to us, we become more proactive in pursuing it? Self-motivation can make all the difference between mediocrity and success, so the more that we should find ways to harness it.

But what is self-motivation really? And why is it so hard to stay motivated?

Simply put, self-motivation is that force that makes you want to do things. It's an essential life skill that makes you want to improve your quality of living. It's that drive that's ingrained in every person's core that makes you want to accomplish something that will leave you with a feeling of deep fulfillment.

I want to share with you my story. My journey of how I got here. For many years, I lived life as any normal person. I got up, went to work, came back home, and slept. Except for the occasional parties here and there, this was pretty much my routine. Until one day, I woke up feeling empty. I didn't know where it was coming from, but at that moment, I remember thinking to myself this isn't the life that I envisioned for myself. Growing up, I always wanted to create an impact on others. I dreamt of being the doctor who will find that cure for cancer, that lawyer who will win the biggest human rights case in the world, the athlete who will win countless Olympic medals, but none of those dreams came true. I wanted to be inspiring people and changing lives, but there I was, several years after, a sad, boring, middle-aged man, with nothing to show for it.

I realized that day that the reason why I wasn't living the life I wanted was because I lacked self-motivation. Even though, as a child, I was always full of dreams. I didn't really do anything to make those dreams come true. I wasn't motivated enough to take the first step to greatness. And I regretted it.

I didn't let the regret get to me. I decided that day that I was going to pick myself up and turn things around. And so, I started reading about self-motivation and putting my own theories to the test. I studied my own behavior (and other people's too), to fully understand how important motivation is in maximizing your potential. What I found out after years of studying and observing changed me completely. This book is the result of all those sleepless nights and endless studying.

If you're lacking direction and have no idea where to go, this is where your journey begins. This book will help you find the direction you're looking for.

If you're lacking focus, this could be a big problem. You don't have to force motivation on yourself. This book will tell you everything you need to know about cultivating it naturally. If you have a dream and you have all the right reasons to pursue it, this book will help you stay focused on it.

If you're lacking in confidence and you want to know how you can take matters into your own hands, this book will teach you how to increase your chances of success. The first step is to believe in yourself; that you're capable of achieving anything you set your mind to. You may not know this yet, but you have all the power in you to reach your full potential.

I hope this book changes your life as much as it has changed mine.

Other priceless variables in the endeavour toward success are **focus,** and **confidence,** these books that have helped are here: **The Power of Focus** and **The Power of Self Confidence.** You can download the eBook for free for a limited time. I am constantly surprised of what people can, or cannot achieve for that matter with the right amount of focus and confidence.

Chapter 1
Creative thought.

Thinking creatively to find what drives you.

What exactly is it that motivates a person to go after a dream? The journey can be difficult, even scary, and many people have died with broken hearts because they weren't able to fulfill their goals. Yet, some people go after their dreams with everything they've got.

Well, according to studies, we are all motivated by different things. Some are motivated by fame, while others are motivated by financial gain. Still others look forward to the feeling of satisfaction from being able to accomplish a lifelong dream. Whatever you're motivated by, is it enough to get you from where you are right now, to the point where you want to be?

Think of that one goal that you want to accomplish more than anything in the world. Now think of the lengths you would be willing to go to reach your goal. If you can't think of any, then you probably don't want it badly enough.

The truth is, we are motivated by what we desire the most. When we want something so bad, we never seem to run out of motivation. But when we're unsure about what we want, there doesn't seem to be much motivation around. The truth is, without that driving force that stirs you up to take action, it would be almost impossible to muster up any motivation. It all begins with purpose.

If you're still on the journey of finding your purpose, there are a few steps you can take to start developing your self-motivation. But first, you need to understand how you're motivated.

According to experts, there are 2 different types of motivation. There's intrinsic motivation, or motivation that comes from within, and there's extrinsic motivation, or motivation that is influenced by external factors. By understanding these 2 types of motivation, you'll gain a better understanding of what drives you.

Intrinsic motivation

Intrinsic or internal motivation mainly deals with the desire you have to do certain things. For whatever reason, you're motivated to do things because it satisfies a longing inside you. People who have strong intrinsic motivation are usually emotionally driven. They do things because of the sense of joy or peace they feel after.

Extrinsic motivation

Extrinsic or external motivation on the other hand is fueled by external factors. You do it because there's a tangible reward at stake. People who have strong extrinsic motivation are often driven by material gain. They do things so that they can impress others with their accomplishments.

People can be influenced by both types of motivation at any point. While one type may have a stronger influence than the other, that doesn't mean that one type is better than the other. It's up to you to know what exactly drives you and use that in developing your self-motivation.

But how do you know exactly if you're intrinsically or extrinsically motivated? I'm sure by now, after reading their basic definitions, you somehow already have an idea of which type you are. But if you're still unsure, here's a quick exercise you can do.

On a piece of paper, write down 10 things that you want most in this world. Try not to overthink this. Just write the first 10 things that come to mind as they come. Don't even rank it. Just get to writing. Once you've written down 10 things, try to categorize them as intrinsic or extrinsic. Samples for intrinsic motivation are joy, pleasure, satisfaction, security, while extrinsic motivations are money, recognition, material things. You are the type that gets the most points. By knowing whether you're intrinsically or extrinsically motivated, you will find the deeper purpose of why you do the things you do.

If there's one thing that can have a huge impact on your self-motivation, it's having a sense of purpose. That sense of purpose is what gets you up from bed in the mornings and gives your life meaning. Without it, you won't have the drive to move forward or do anything with your life. Finding out is the first step to greatness.

How to find your purpose in life

Ask the right questions

While finding your purpose is journey, it isn't rocket science. You just need to ask yourself the right questions if you want to uncover what really drives you. One good question that you can ask yourself is: "If money wasn't an issue, what would you choose to do for the rest of your life?" By answering this simple question, you'll start to see the things that really matters to you.

Go back to your childhood for clues

Another way to uncover your purpose in life is to remember the things you did when you were a child that gave you so much joy. Perhaps, you loved to write stories, or you had an unexplainable fascination for bugs. Try to think of the activities that you really enjoyed before the pressures of growing up got to you. These memories from childhood, both good and bad, might just help you find your purpose now that you're an adult.

Consult close family and friends for validation

You can also ask help from your closest family and friends for insight. Assuming that these people know you well and have been with you on your journey, you might just get some interesting feedback on what they think your passions could be. They could offer you outsider perspective and might even help you realize some things that you're still not aware of at this point.

Create something

When all else fails and you still find yourself stuck, the best thing you can do is to go out there and try to create something. You can also try to think of something that you can make that would make you happy. Even if you don't think you'll be particularly good at it, don't be afraid to give it a try. It can be anything from crafts to digital media, and even random write-ups. Let your creative side take over, even just once, and you might just discover something inside you that you never knew you had before.

Many people underestimate the value of creative thinking in finding one's purpose. Personally, I used to think that creativity and imagination had nothing to do with finding my purpose in life. I didn't consider myself to be creative like the other kids when I was growing up, so I didn't put much effort into being creative. I didn't paint, or sing, or act in any school play, so I quickly dismissed creativity as being 'not my thing'. But when I started to think about my purpose, that's when I realized that creativity plays a huge role in finding your purpose and developing self-motivation. It's only when I allowed that first spark of creativity to overwhelm me, that I finally realized my purpose.

If you're ready to give creative thinking a try, follow these 3 easy steps:

Pursue the unknown

Getting stuck in a routine kills creativity. Break away from your routine by doing something that is in unfamiliar territory for you. Don't be afraid to pursue the unknown. Sign up for a new class or take a trip to a place you've never been before. Talk to a person you've just met or read a book that you wouldn't normally read. Step out of your comfort zone to expand your mind.

Find your inspiration

Inspiration can come in many forms. For some, it's music, while for others, it's being in nature. Some people find inspiration in paintings and art, and there are those who are inspired by people and their stories. Take time out from your busy schedule to find what inspires you. But how do you know if it's your inspiration? Simple. If it stimulates you to create something out of it, then you've found something that ignites your creativity.

Work your imagination

Working on your imagination is a good way to enhance your creative thinking. Just like with major muscles in your body, working on your imagination will help strengthen creativity. The more you visualize or imagine, the more that you want to create it. And the stronger that drive to create something, the better your self-motivation will be. That's how powerful your mind can be. If you can imagine it, there's a chance that you can make it.

Chapter 2
Develop a big picture

Developing a big picture mindset

Success begins with one thought. When this thought is cultivated and given space to grow, that's when you start to see the big picture. For most of us, it's easier to focus on details. It's easy to get stuck in the day to day because we believe this is what we need to do to make progress. But what we fail to see is that looking at the big picture is just as important as the everyday details. We need to keep our sights on the big picture for the everyday details to make sense.

The problem with focusing on the details too much is that it stops you from reaching your full potential. Sure, you might be able to finish off your task list, but you'll have to do it all over again tomorrow. You might work countless hours on a project just to get it done, but I'm pretty sure nothing's going to change much on your next project. With no greater purpose or passion to fuel you, getting stuck in the details is a surefire way to lose self-motivation.

So what difference does seeing the big picture make in developing your self-motivation? Let me tell you that it makes a huge difference. For one, seeing the big picture helps you stay on the right track. Without an end goal in mind, it's hard to see whether you're making any progress in what you set out to do. Having a big picture mindset will also help you redirect your course if you find that there are changes around you. Since you're not caught up in the details, you'll see other opportunities that you can take. You'll be motivated to move forward even with all the challenges and difficulties around you.

If you want to see the importance of looking at the big picture, imagine a single leaf falling from a tree. On its own, there's really nothing special about this leaf. It's just going to fall to the ground and that will be the end of that. Now imagine that you're in the middle of autumn and you see countless leaves of different colors fall all at the same time. Together, all these leaves make a surreal picture that shows off the beauty of nature. If you're going to focus on just one leaf, there's really not much to see. But if you look at the big picture, you'll be amazed by the beauty before you.

The sad thing is, seeing the big picture is not always easy. It's a skill that we must intentionally cultivate on a daily basis. We need to put effort into it since most of us have been trained to pay more attention to the details. But once it becomes a habit, it gets much easier to overcome the barriers that are stopping us from seeing the big picture. It's just a matter of knowing what limiting habits are stopping you and taking the necessary action to counter that.

Limiting Habits

- Procrastinating holds you back from accomplishing your goals.
- Negative thinking pushes you to only see the negative in all situations
- Playing the blame game and making excuses makes you feel like you're not responsible for your actions
- Overthinking things not only wastes your energy, but your time as well
- Focusing on shallow issues distracts from seeing the things that truly matter
- Striving for perfection forces you to do things over and over again in the hopes that you'll achieve the impossible.
- Short-term thinking blinds you from the opportunities that lie ahead

Are any of these habits hindering you from seeing the big picture? Are they stopping you from living out your full potential? Be real with yourself and create an action plan today that will help you see much clearer. This way, you'll be able to differentiate big picture goals that you can reach from unrealistic goals that are just impossible to achieve.

Having a big picture goal is one of the best ways to keep yourself motivated. By taking a step back to see a big picture that you want to achieve, you become more invested into the process. As long as you set realistic goals, no matter how big they may seem right now, you have a high chance of making them come true.

But of course, your success still depends on the goals you set. Setting goals that are just impossible to reach is only going to end in disappointment and frustration. So, you need to know how to set big picture goals that are just barely out of your reach.

What exactly am I talking about here?

Let's say you've always wanted to become an astronaut and explore the great beyond. Since being an astronaut requires a high level of expertise, there's no way that you'll be sent to space without the right education or the rigorous training. You can set your goal to become an astronaut, but without the credentials, your goal will remain an impossible goal.

On the other hand, if your goal is to be one of the top 10 online marketing experts, and you already have the basic credentials, even if it may seem unlikely right now, it's not impossible. As long as you're ready to put in the hours to learning, testing, applying different online marketing techniques, then eventually, your hard work will pay off. You'll become one of the best because you were smart enough to work with what you already have. This is what a goal that is barely within your reach looks like. You may be far from achieving your goal, but it's not impossible for you to get there.

As I've mentioned earlier, having a big picture mindset is a habit that you need to develop. While it may seem a bit challenging in the beginning, over time, it will feel like second nature to you. Here's what you can do to cultivate the habit.

1. Watch your language

The words you say reflects your thoughts so if you're constantly criticizing and complaining, then that's basically what's in your heart. Instead of focusing on the negative, make it a habit to use positive and empowering words, especially when talking about yourself.

2. Think ahead

The only way that you'll be able to see the big picture is by thinking ahead. People with the big picture mindset make sure that they're a few steps ahead. They look at life as a game of chess, where being several moves ahead is crucial.

3. Focus on solutions

Instead of focusing on the problems, divert your thought to the solutions. Seeing the big picture is all about finding ideas and solutions to whatever could be standing in the way of your success. By seeing the big picture, you're opening yourself to alternative solutions that may have never crossed your mind before.

4. Step out of your comfort zone

Don't ever settle for less. This is your time to expand your horizons and step out of your comfort zone. Don't be afraid to test your limits and work your imagination. Free your mind and allow it to think big. Life is too short for you to not take risks.

5. Believe

Seeing the big picture requires unshakeable belief because without faith, you won't be motivated to turn your wildest dreams into reality. Believe that you hold your future in your hands and that you're capable of doing whatever it takes to live the life you've always dreamed of.

How does big picture thinking fuel keep us motivated? Focusing on the big picture helps us develop willpower and resilience. It's hard to move forward when you have no vision of what lies ahead. When you can't see how the circumstances connect or the greater purpose of it all, it's hard to gather the willpower to move forward. Even the smallest goals will seem unreachable.

Chapter 3
SMART goals

Setting SMART goals

We've all heard this before. Setting goals is the first step to reach success. Without goals, you won't have anything to aim for. But it's not enough that you set goals and leave it at that. You need to set SMART goals. The truth is, not all goals are the same. Some goals are fleeting, while others will propel you to greatness. It all depends on how you set up your goal. This is why setting goals according to the SMART guidelines is vital. SMART goals are goals that are designed to increase your chances of success.

But first, what is a goal anyway?

A goal is an objective that you set out for yourself to achieve. Goals can be small, like exercising for 30 minutes a day, and they can be big, like landing that promotion after months of hard work. Having goals, whether big or small, can be very beneficial. That's if you set goals that give your life meaning and push you to move towards bigger better things.

The common mistake that many people make when setting goals is they often set goals that are not achievable. Not just hard to achieve, but downright impossible to achieve. While setting larger than life goals can be inspiring, they can often end up in disappointment and frustration. They can also be hard to gauge and measure, making it very challenging to track real progress.

Setting SMART goals is the only way to go if you want to get the maximum benefit from them. Follow these SMART principles in writing down your goals and set yourself up for success.

Specific

When setting goals, try to be as specific as you can be. Have a clear and concise goal that you can aim for. Instead of saying "I want to read more books", you can say "I want to finish 10 books by the end of June". By being more specific with your goals, you're conditioning your mind to achieve them.

Measurable

One of the most important factors in keeping yourself motivated is to track the progress of your goals. Set milestones that are connected to your goals and celebrate them when you reach these milestones. If you don't get to your milestones, don't fret! Take this time to reevaluate your goals. Setting goals that can be evaluated and measured is a great way to check if you're still on the right track.

Achievable

As mentioned earlier, too many people make the mistake of setting goals that are not very realistic. While these goals may motivate you in the beginning, it's easy to give up on them when the going gets tough. Don't aim for the impossible, aim for the achievable. One way to gauge whether a goal is achievable or not is to try to envision yourself at that point you've achieved it. If you just don't see it happening, then you might need to go back to the drawing board.

Relevant

Not all goals are going to be relevant. There are some that may seem right at the moment but will lose its relevance in a few weeks' time. So, if you goal isn't relevant to your greater purpose, then achieving them may only be meaningless. Your goals should create a positive effect in your life in order to be worth your time and effort. If your goals don't align with your mission or doesn't align with your other goals to some degree, they might not be worth pursuing.

Time-bound

Lastly, set goals with a time element to them. Instead of saying "I want to get back into shape," it's better to say, "I want to lose 15 lbs. in the next 6 months." You'll be more motivated to reach your goal because there's a deadline. Just like when you set specific goals, setting time-bound goals conditions your mind to achieve them.

Writing down your goals can be a bit tricky. It can also be frustrating for some. But with this guide, you'll be writing goals with an achiever mindset in no time.

And it's that achiever mindset that will bring you to your success. Nothing feels as great as finally getting to that point where you reached a goal. The high that you get when you can finally say "you did it!" is already a reward on its own. But that doesn't mean that you should only focus on getting easy wins. You also need to dig deep and focus on the meaning of it all.

Your goals should inspire you to become the best version of yourself. For your goals to be a source of motivation, they should be rooted on your deeper purpose and meaning. They should mean so much to you that you sometimes feel like you can't end the day without doing something that is connected towards that goal. Your goals should ignite a passion in you to keep you motivated.

Here's what you need to remember about goals - it's very rare that you'll be able to accomplish them without putting in the time or effort. While this thought can be motivating to some degree, it can also be very intimidating. You may have set all the right objectives and created an action plan, but if you don't have an idea where to even begin, then you'll only end up procrastinating.

Your goal and action plan are two completely different things. To maximize their potential, you need to break your goals into actionable chunks. This will also help you break down your vague goals and turn them into something more concrete.

To break your goals into actionable chunks, you'll need to work backwards from your goal. So, let's say, your goal is to start your own business within the year. You need to think of the things you need to do to make this happen. Have you chosen a product or service to offer? Who are your customers? How are you going to brand your business? You'll also need to sort out the legalities of starting a business. What kind of permit do you need? Where are you getting these permits from?

After you break down your goal into chunks, see if these chunks can be broken down further to smaller chunks. This will help you create a task list and set a timeframe for your goal.

Setting goals is basically a never-ending learning experience. Even though it can be very challenging sometimes, there's a lot to learn from the process. But don't worry. The more you do it, the better you'll be at it. But you should also be willing to evaluate where you are in the journey so that you can change your course if needed.

Goal setting is one of the most effective ways to develop self-motivation. Add this to hard work and a clear vision of yourself, and you'll be unstoppable.

Chapter 4
Reflective Thinking

Thinking back to get ahead

They say that by taking the first step towards your goal, you've already won half the battle. I believe the other half is trying to stay motivated as you do what needs to be done to get to where you want to be. We all have the tendency to lose motivation, especially when we're forced to do the same thing over and over again. The everyday routine can get boring quickly and leave you feeling demotivated.

Having a routine per se isn't bad. It gives you a sense of stability and order in your day. In fact, there are some people who thrive quite well in their routines. A well-balanced routine can be freeing for some as it allows them to slow down and conserve their brain space and energy for bigger projects. But when a routine turns unhealthy and hinders you from growing, that's when it gets a bit tricky. If you feel like your routine is making you complacent and lazy, it's time to change it up. Are you having a hard time staying focused on your goal? One way that could motivate you is to set a deadline.

I know we all dread that word. Trying to beat the deadline can be very stressful for some. But deadlines can also help you stay on track. Having a deadline is one of the most effective ways to get motivation. And once you realize that you're capable of finishing a task within the time frame, the feeling of accomplishment that you get after is incomparable.

You can set deadlines for just about anything when you start to feel like you're losing motivation. And announcing it to others makes the deadline even more powerful. You'll be motivated to give it all you've got because not meeting the deadline can be a reflection of your character. It can feel as bad as breaking a promise.

Another way to stay motivated is to track your progress. Setting a goal or a set destination isn't enough. You need to have a way to track where you are on your journey. Failing to track your progress, you won't have a way to know if you're getting closer to or farther from where you want to be. And let me tell you, it's hard to keep motivated when you feel like you're running around in circles and not making any real progress. It's not enough to keep mental tabs. Keeping a journal is a powerful tool to help you stay focused on your goals. Here are a few journaling tips to help you track your progress.

- Choose a journal that works for you. It really doesn't matter what kind of journal you use, as long as it works for you. Whether you prefer to take the traditional route and use a notebook, or if you're more tech savvy and work better on your mobile, the medium is completely up to you. You should be able to take your journal with you anywhere so make sure that it's convenient and compact.

- Make journaling a part of your daily routine. For journaling to work for you, consistency is key. Make it a part of your daily routine by setting a specific time for it. You can work on this any time of the day, as long as you have a clear mind when you do. Some people prefer to do it first thing in the morning, while others are more comfortable doing in at night before they go to sleep.

- Try not to miss a day. Again, to take full advantage of this tool, you need to be consistent at it. While it can be hard to journal every day when you have a busy schedule, remember that it only takes a few minutes of your time. You don't have to write a lengthy entry when you really don't have the time. A short note is enough as long as you make that note count.

- Include motivational quotes. Be inspired by other people's journeys and include motivational quotes in your journal. These quotes will remind you to keep pushing forward even when the going gets tough. Hey! If they were able to get through their challenges and achieve their goals, so can you!

- Keep your journal for 'your eyes only'. Unless you want to show your journal to an accountability person who you really trust, then by all means. But if you think that you're not ready to let other people know about what you're going through, that's perfectly fine. Keep your journal somewhere safe or if you're journaling on your mobile, don't forget to set a password to protect the file.

Tracking your progress using a journal requires both forward thinking and reflective thinking. There should be a good balance when looking towards your future and looking back at your past. We all know how forward thinking can help boost motivation, but how can reflective thinking help?

Reflective thinking is looking back to your experiences and using them as motivation to move forward. It's looking back to see what the experience has taught you, so you can make better choices in the future. Reflective thinking isn't automatic and will require time and effort to practice, but once you develop this skill, it can expand your mind and help you change how you live your life. So how do you develop this very important skill? Here are 6 simple steps you need to follow.

Ways you develop your reflective thinking

1. Read, read, and read! Be a voracious reader and read a wide range of topics.

Even if there are some topics that you're not particularly interested in, take the chance to learn something new.

2. Ask people questions. Engage others into conversation by asking thought provoking questions. Just make sure that your questions aren't offensive in any way.

3. Watch and be mindful of what's going on around you. Observe people and find out how things are connected to each other.

4. Feel your emotions. Pay attention to what you're feeling. Don't allow negative emotions to control you. If you're always being pulled down by your negative thought processes and feelings, find healthy ways to cope emotionally.

5. Talk it out. Don't be afraid to share your views and experiences with others. Other people can also learn from what you've been through and what you're

currently working on so work on keeping the communication cycle going.

6. Think of your journey so far. Try to look for opportunities for improvement. If you made mistakes in the past, think of how you'll be able to avoid making the same mistakes in the future.

Aside from fueling your motivation, reflective thinking can also help you identify the factors that are hindering you from reaching your goals. Whether you have fallen out of track or you're dealing with distractions, thinking reflectively can help you adjust your strategy and maintain your focus. By looking back with unbiased eyes, you'll be able to explore your mind to find the right solutions to your problems. It will teach you to deal with difficult situations with calm and grace.

Chapter 5
Shared goal or accountability

Setting Accountability

Do you ever wonder what sets successful people apart from the rest of the world? What could they be doing that they're able to hit their goals every time? I used to lay awake at night wondering what it could be. In my life, I've witnessed many people around me set goals and actually reach those goals. I admit that at some point, it made me jealous. Whatever it is that made them successful - I wanted to have it. So, I started to observe them in the hopes that I would eventually uncover their secret. What I found out was surprising to say the least.

Turns out, what made them successful wasn't such a big secret after all. Actually, it was out in the open, and free for everyone to see. They were successful because they practiced accountability with the right people.

Being accountable to someone else is one of the most effective ways to stay motivated. We are after all, social by nature. Studies show that people who choose to be accountable to an exercise buddy are more likely to show up at the gym and actually work out. Accountability offers a healthy form of peer pressure that can effectively motivate a person to act on a promise or commitment. The closer the bond there is between the two people, the stronger their influence will be on each other. So, you can expect real progress to happen when they're both working towards the same goal.

It's not a hierarchical relationship (parent-child, boss-employee) that will create the biggest impact in a person's success. Rather it's the peer to peer relationship that seems to be more effective in motivating a person to really go after their dreams. When there's collaboration between two people who respect and like each other, the tedious journey towards success becomes much more bearable.

So how do you find someone you can be accountable to? Who makes the best accountability partners? Here are some tips on how you can start an accountability relationship.

- Choose someone you already have a good relationship with. You can't have an accountability relationship with someone you don't trust. Whether it's someone from your family or a close friend, find someone you can talk to easily. While it can be difficult for some people to open up, especially those who have experienced some form of trauma in the past, having an accountability partner who has gone through a similar experience can really help. Choose someone who you can relate to. Try not to discredit someone just because you have different personalities.

- Tell them about your goals. Since the whole point of starting an accountability relationship is to have someone support you while you reach your goals, telling them about what exactly it is that you're aiming for is a surefire way to make sure that you're on the same page. Don't be afraid to get honest about your goals. No matter how big or small they are, your accountability partner will be happy to hear it from you.

- Let them in on your action plan. And be specific when telling them about the details. By sharing your plan with them, you're giving them a chance to take part in your journey, so be open to their suggestions. Don't quickly dismiss their advice, especially if it's something that you don't agree with in the first place. Let them voice their concerns. They might be seeing a side that you're not seeing.

- Be consistent in meeting up. Try to set a regular schedule where you can talk about your goals. You don't have to meet face to face each time, as long as you find a way to communicate regularly. Some people have turned to Skype or Facebook to speak with their accountabilities. Don't let your busy schedule get in the way of your accountability sessions. Sometimes a simple phone call would be enough.

- Track your progress together. The best part about being accountable to someone is that you know you have someone who will be with you every step of the way. Make sure that you revisit strategies and goals with your accountability partner once in a while just to make sure that you're still on track.

When you become accountable to someone else, you increase your chances of reaching your goals and at the same time, you get the chance to develop a healthy and transparent relationship with someone else. But the benefits don't end there. You also become a better and more focused person over time.

Accountability keeps you stable. Even when there are a million and one things distracting you, it won't affect you so much because you're focused on reaching your goals.

Accountability makes you more responsible. When you work with someone else, you become more invested in the goal. You're more open to taking on more responsibilities because you don't want to let your accountability person down.

Accountability gives you space to be more mindful. And because you have someone to bounce your ideas off, you silence the inner critic in you. You have more opportunities to really think things through.

An accountability person is someone who will tell you what you need to hear and not what you want to hear. And if you put the effort in developing a true accountable relationship with this person, you'll always have someone who will act as your mentor as you chase your dreams. Doesn't it feel great to know that there is someone out there who wants you to succeed? If that's not motivation enough to get you going, I don't know what is.

At the end of the day, you are more likely to act on your goals when you know that there's someone else watching over you and cheering you on your way. With strong accountability, you'll think twice about ever giving up.

Chapter 6
Bring value to others

Motivating others to motivate yourself

Imagine this. It's late at night, you're working on a project, and the only form of social interaction you have is through Facebook. You're tired, maybe even a little bit frustrated, and on the verge of giving up because no matter what you do, you can't seem to make any significant progress on the project. If this scenario feels all too familiar, then here's a lesser known tip that could help you boost your self-motivation. Try motivating the people around you.

Motivating others to get a little motivation for yourself may seem counterintuitive. After all, how can you give something that you don't have? But according to experts, motivating the people around you, most especially those who are part of your team, will not just motivate you, it can also give you a better chance at achieving your goals. When you motivate others towards their goals, they become more productive and easier to work with. And when you start to see others working tirelessly towards their goals, it's hard not to replicate their actions.

The ability to motivate others is crucial to your success because no one on this earth can achieve anything on their own. Whether you admit it or not, we can all benefit from each other.

The benefits of being part of a team

Intellectual stimulation
One of the great things about being part of a team is that it gives you access to unlimited

ideas. Working with others gives you access to opportunities to learn from others and share different ideas. You get the chance to see things through a different perspective, so you're not limited to your own way of thinking.

Efficient process

Being part of a team also makes any and all processes more efficient. You can finish tasks faster when there are others working with you. Mistakes will also be quickly identified since yours is not the only pair of eyes checking the output. What's more, when you're around people who is headed towards the same goal as you, you can feed off each other's drive.

Strength in numbers

You'll also find that you're stronger when you're working with a team. When you're working with other people, you can take advantage of each other's strengths. Projects become more manageable since each individual will only need to work on the task that they can take on. When you're surrounded by people who have complementary skills, there's nothing that you won't be able to achieve.

We all have that longing to belong to a community where we can help each other out. This is why, when you motivate others to reach their goals, they'll be able to do their part and you won't feel frustrated by lazy or unproductive people. After all, you are the company that you keep. When you're surrounded by people who are passionate about what they do, that can quickly catch on to you. Motivation can be very contagious.

5 ways to motivate others

Take the role of listener
Most people have this notion that motivation comes with flowery words and lengthy speeches, but this doesn't always apply. Sometimes it's better to just listen to what others want to do before you give a motivational speech. By knowing what the

other person's goals are, you'll be able to create a connection and you'll know the right words to say.

Ask the right questions

Asking the right questions can also help you become a better motivator. When you ask questions, you show interest in others, which then makes it easier for them to open up to you. Again, it's all about creating a connection between you and the person you want to motivate.

Be there from the very beginning

Motivating others doesn't end with the motivational speeches. It's not enough that you say the right words, make the effort to be there from the very beginning of their journey. Even if you can't offer much, be there to offer support, advice, or anything that they may need that you're capable of giving. Asking how you can help may not seem much, but it's a good way to motivate the other person to start.

Don't be a downer, be an encourager

Whatever happens, always make the choice to be an encourager. Most people already have that inner critic inside their head that they can't shut out, so they don't need you to play that part. Realizing a dream can be very scary for some people but having an encourager makes taking the first step much easier.

Share the dream

Share your own dreams and give the person you're motivating a glimpse into your own journey towards your goals. Even though your dreams may seem far at the moment, connecting your dreams to your future reality can help you feel motivated towards reaching them.

When you motivate and others around you to reaching for their goals, you'll also feel more passionate about reaching yours. Igniting motivation in others contributes to a positive attitude, which you can leverage to your success.

To achieve positive results, you need to have a positive attitude. It's your attitude that dictates how you look at the world. If you have a negative attitude towards the world, then all you will see are the negative things, and this will affect your motivation.

But if you have a positive attitude towards the world, you'll see the good in everything, even when the challenges come. Even if trials come to test you, you'll be able to carry on. When you have a positive attitude, no matter how badly you get hit, you'll still be in good spirits.

So how do you develop a positive attitude? By shifting your thoughts. Yes, it takes work, but making the conscious effort to think positive thoughts is the only way to overcome a negative attitude. You can't just choose to stop being negative and expect a change instantly. It's a process where you need to replace a bad habit with a good habit. So, whenever you feel like you're being run by your negative thoughts, doing these 3 steps will help you shift those thoughts.

1. Quiet down and just breathe. The world can be a very noisy place. With so much going on, it's very rare that there will be moments where you can just quiet down and breathe. This is why you need to be intentional about getting your 'quiet time', quieting your mind and breathing deep breaths can help open your mind and make it more receptive to positive thoughts. Don't let the distractions get the best of you.

2. Be mindful of your thoughts because your thoughts can have power over you. Your thoughts can ignite feelings and these feelings can lead you to act and behave a certain way. If you start off your day with bad thoughts, you're basically setting yourself up to have a

bad day. By being mindful over your thoughts, you're taking matters into your own hands.

3. Write a gratitude list. There's always something to be grateful for no matter what you're going through. Start your day right by writing down a gratitude list. Every day, before you do anything else, write down 5 things that you're genuinely grateful for. Keeping a small journal with all the things you're grateful is an effective way to shift your thoughts and help you cultivate a positive mindset.

Chapter 7
Patience and focus

Developing patience and refocusing on the big picture

Patience, they say, is a virtue. Unfortunately, it was a virtue I just didn't have. I absolutely hated waiting, and I often became very frustrated when faced with delays. I was often stressed and didn't take the time to think things through. I would rush into projects, meetings, even relationships, because I had the "I want it now and I want it fast" mentality. In simple words, I was restless and was controlled by my impulses.

You may think, "Yeah, but isn't that a good thing? Doesn't that make you more efficient than others?" Well, that's what I thought too until it started to affect my motivation. I started to lose it when I almost got fired from my job. You see, at that time, I easily got burned out when confronted with large tasks because I wanted to finish them as fast as I could. I lost a lot of good opportunities because I didn't like to wait. And because I was rushing from one task to another, I failed to produce quality output.

Have you ever taken the time to think about what patience really is and how it can create a positive impact on your life?

Having patience is that innate ability in all humans, to wait for something without becoming agitated. It's also being able to control one's emotions and restlessness for the greater good. While some people may have more patience than others, we all possess this ability. And because having patience is more of ability rather than a trait, it can be developed. So, there's really no excuse for you not to be patient.

To be patient, you need to have a proactive nature. This means that you need to be involved and give it your full attention. In achieving your goals, some things can't be rushed. Some things require more time and effort before you can see any progress. This is why long-term commitment is crucial on your part. Without patience, it will be hard for you to follow through.

Patience and self-motivation work hand in hand simply because without patience, it's hard to stay motivated. You'll end up giving up before you even start because you can't stand to wait, or you can't cope with the challenges. Could you imagine what kind of world we would be living in if Edison gave up on the idea of the light bulb after his first failed attempt, or if Alexander Graham Bell didn't put in years of work to invent the telephone?

But I'm already getting ahead of myself here. Let's talk about how patience can have a positive impact on us normal people.

Benefits of having patience

Improved relationships
Developing your capacity to be more patient is one the best things you can do to improve the quality of your relationships. Why? It is because deep inside us all, we respect people who display patience. When you are patient, you don't get easily frustrated with people so they're more likely to look to you for support and advice.

Clarity

You begin to see things more clearly because you can set aside your emotional impulses. Having patience gives you a deeper understanding of everything that's going on around you. You then become more aware of how different factors are connected and what you can do to improve your situation. Patience helps you enhance your problem-solving ability because you can think clearer without getting emotionally riled up.

Less stress

And because you understand the value of waiting, you can slow down and let things out of your control unfold on their own. You don't get easily fazed by obstacles anymore because you're more focused on reaching your goals.

By having patience, you'll be more prepared to handle the big challenges that are yet to come. You'll see that you're happier and healthier because you can simply wait for the right opportunities to come. You don't have that need to control the circumstances anymore.

So how do you develop patience? Here are a few things I can suggest. Before I understood the real value of patience, I was a very impatient person so if these tips worked on me, I'm 100% confident that they will also work for you.

5 ways develop patience

Slow down

Rushing around and trying to hurry things up is not what's going to get you the results you want. Learn to slow down and let things happen in their own time. If stress is starting to overwhelm you, make it a habit to take deep breaths before you act. Let's say you're caught in heavy traffic or the line at the grocery store is taking too long, the best way to respond to situations that are beyond your control is to take deep breaths There's really nothing you can do to move things along faster so don't stress over it.

Make patience your goal - everyday!
Be intentional in practicing patience every day. The reason why most of us are impatient is because we don't put much effort into practicing patience. Be more mindful and try living in the moment. Look for opportunities where you can practice patience. Whether it's waiting in line for your

coffee or spending time with your hyperactive children with limited attention spans, always choose patience as your response. Developing patience is pretty much like working out your body because you need to put effort and persistence in it.

Think before you speak

For many people, this can be difficult. Often times, we blurt out the first thing that comes to our minds without thinking it through. This can lead to conflict and sometimes, even fractured relationships. This is why, before you say anything, practice thinking before speaking. Pause for a second and think of what you're going to say. What do you want to accomplish with your words? Do you use your words to build someone up or break them down? By pausing before you speak, you become better at using your words for good and you won't end up offending or hurting people.

Delay gratification

Are you familiar with the marshmallow test? From that study, we see that the children, who delayed gratification and waited for the second marshmallow, grew up to become more successful adults than the children who quickly ate their marshmallow. If you think you're not the type who has that same level of self-control, don't worry, you still have time to work on it. The next time you reach for a second beer, order a dessert, or look online to buy something, take a few seconds to think if you badly need it. Ask yourself, what satisfaction do you gain from it? Delaying gratification not only helps you be more patient, but it will also save you a lot of money in the long run.

Create more

Creativity is not just for helping you express yourself, it can also lead you to opportunities to practice patience. By taking on a form of art and turning it into a hobby, like painting, sketching, or even crafting, you learn to persevere more. Most of the time the process of creating something can be frustrating. When ideas don't seem to click, or when your technique doesn't get you the results you want, you'll need tons of patience to see your ideas come to life. Creating more gives you the patience to express your ideas to their physical form.

With patience, it will be easier for you to focus on your goals, especially the big ones that seem out of your reach at this moment. Just remember to hang in there. After all, good things come to those who wait.

Conclusion

So, there you have it. I hope this book helps you become a more self-motivated person out to make your dreams come true.

I hope that whatever you set out to accomplish, you will do it to the best of your abilities. Remember, there is no short cut to achieving your goals. It's up to you to find the drive to improve yourself, take the necessary steps, and increase your chances of real success. While support from family and friends are always welcome, at the end of the day, it's all on you.

By developing self-motivation and keeping your eyes on the big picture, get ready to accomplish things that are beyond your imagination.

I wish you joy, peace, and success in all your endeavors!

www.ingramcontent.com/pod-product-compliance
Lightning Source LLC
Chambersburg PA
CBHW070215230526
45471CB00002B/956